Single, Saved, and Having Sex

With a look at why do saved Married People Cheat?

Vernice (Vern) Haliburton

AuthorHouse™
1663 Liberty Drive
Bloomington, IN 47403
www.authorhouse.com
Phone: 1-800-839-8640

© 2011 Vernice (Vern) Haliburton. All rights reserved.

No part of this book may be reproduced, stored in
a retrieval system, or transmitted by any means
without the written permission of the author.

First published by AuthorHouse 11/1/2011

ISBN: 978-1-4670-7293-9 (sc)
ISBN: 978-1-4670-7292-2 (e)

Library of Congress Control Number: 2011919516

Printed in the United States of America

Any people depicted in stock imagery provided by Thinkstock are models,
and such images are being used for illustrative purposes only.
Certain stock imagery © Thinkstock.

This book is printed on acid-free paper.

Because of the dynamic nature of the Internet, any web addresses or
links contained in this book may have changed since publication and
may no longer be valid. The views expressed in this work are solely those
of the author and do not necessarily reflect the views of the publisher,
and the publisher hereby disclaims any responsibility for them.

Chapter 1

MY POINT OF VIEW AS A MOTHER

On June 8, 2010, my mother, Lona Mae Conley, passed away in her sleep from a heart attack—at least, that's what the death certificate said. My mother never had heart problems to our knowledge; however, she did have high blood pressure, diabetes, high cholesterol, COPD, osteoporosis, and arthritis. It wasn't until my mother passed away that we learned she had used many different last names in her past, and the grandfather's name that we grew up knowing was not the name on her birth certificate. My mother never spoke of her parents except to say that they died and left her as a young girl. I never saw a single picture of my grandparents or heard their names. From time to time we would ask her to share some information about them, and each time that small three-minute conversation would bring my mom so much pain that there would be no more conversations for another five or ten years. My three sisters and I were told that my grandmother died when my mom was sixteen years old, so I wonder who taught her about the facts of life? How did she learn what sex and love was all about? My older sibling was born to my mother when my mom was twenty years old. I was her twenty-fifth birthday present, as her birthday was on March 10, 1959, and I came into this world on March 14, 1959. Whom was I born to and where was my daddy? There was a man's name on my birth certificate when I was born, but by the time I turned eighteen and needed a copy of it, the name had been replaced by the words "legally omitted."

I grew up in Blue Island, Illinois, in a standard American home. I had a mother and a father and three sisters, two older and one younger. For most of my early years, I was consumed with anger and hate. It wasn't until I put away my childhood rape issues that I gained controlled of that anger. The interesting thing about being molested as a child from ages seven through twelve is that I knew what was happening to me was wrong and painful and I told; I told everybody who would listen, including my mother. Her only response to me was, and I quote, "I have to work and you have to stay with them after school; what do you expect me to do?"

In today's society, that person would have been arrested and convicted of child molestation and become registered with the local authorities and my parents charged with child abuse or neglect. But back then, children weren't respected and no one listened to anything they had to say. Something like that was considered hush-

hush, as it would bring shame to the family. Healing wasn't an issue or even a thought; keeping the family secret was all that was important.

I was thirty-five years old before I could confront my mom about that, and it was the best thing that ever happened for our relationship. She could never apologize for her role or for not protecting me as her child, but she did acknowledge that she knew he was doing those things to me and said he should have never done that. That was good enough for me; at that point I was able to forgive and release her, and she was able to forgive herself. That is only one story of my childhood household that makes me question who taught Mom about love and sex. I can remember clearly one of my friends asking their mother for birth control pills when she was sixteen years old, and her mom went crazy, screaming, "You don't need any birth control pills! What are you going to do with birth control pills? Are you kidding me?" That was not a pretty scene. Let me just digress for one moment, mothers—if your sixteen-year-old son or daughter asks you for birth control, trust me, he or she knows what to do with it. That is not the time to bury your head in the sand. That is the time to pick up the phone, make a doctor's appointment, and then have that all-important heart-to-heart, non-confrontational talk with your child.

We were a church-going family; in fact, it seemed like we were at the church every time the doors opened. We did the Christmas plays and had our Easter speeches; we sang in the choir and worked on the junior usher board and had the car washes and sold chicken dinners for the building fund. There was Sunday school, vacation Bible school, pastor's anniversaries, church anniversaries, communion Sunday, and on and on. It wasn't just us; it was all our friends too. Whether it was at my church or another, the entire neighborhood did it Sunday in and Sunday out. We did the church thing faithfully, but was God in any of it? Did we or our parents really know Jesus? Did they have a relationship with him? Did we? Or were we all just doing what was expected of us? My mother and father (whom I learned was my stepfather at age of twelve) were married to each other (so they said) for over forty years. They always said it was "over forty," which is kind of understand able since my younger sister, who was their only biological child together, is now well over forty. He passed away about thirteen years before Mom, and I went to Social Security with her to handle some paperwork. I learned that they did not marry until 1974. What? How could that be when the youngest girl was born in 1962? In kindergarten I had known him as my dad, so that meant they lived together out of wedlock all those years, and yet she freaked out when we we spoke of birth control. My mom lived her entire life with a lot of secrets. Some were revealed when my dad passed away, and others upon her passing. Only God knows how many she took to her grave. I can't help but wonder if all those secrets were the real reason for the heart attack. Years and years of holding all that in, not being honest with herself; I guess that would make it hard to be open, honest, and free with her children. May you rest in peace, Mom. If you know me—I mean really know me—and knew my mother, you know that I look just like her. It is almost spooky; as I age I look more and more like her. Often when I get up in the morning and look in the mirror, I have to tell her to please get out of my mirror. I could pass for her twin sister, and I have (or had) a lot of the same habits as her—too many to name. Still, I refuse to bury my head in the sand about who I am, what I have done, and what I want my only daughter to know about me and sex.

My mother worked in the same hospital as a nursing assistant for over thirty years, and she never once spoke to me about sex and boys except to ask me once when I was nineteen why I wasn't dating. She didn't talk to me about my menstrual cycle, ovulation, cramps, or anything else about my body. I was fourteen years old wearing a size 40D bra, which is a lot for a little girl to carry, and man was I teased and talked about a lot for that. When I turned twenty-seven, I had those suckers reduced. You have no idea how hard it is to carry those things around——the shoulder and back pain is ridiculous. Many women pay big bucks to get what I paid big bucks to get rid of.

A lot about who I am, what I feel, and how I think has changed since I lost my mother. I absolutely refuse to carry on her tradition of holding back and holding in those things that a mother and daughter should share. Actually, since my child was born, way before Mom passed, I made a vow that no topic would ever be off limits. Whatever she came to me with, I would handle without shock or embrassement and most of all without ridiculous answers that some might call age appropriate. I can remember a time in the grocery store my daughter was scratching her vagina, I guess she was about five years old, and this old white lady looked down at her and said so sweetly, "Oh honey, your cookie is itching." My daughter looked back at her with this strange expression as if she had no idea what the lady was saying, so the women repeated it. My daughter looked down at her hands and said, "I don't have a cookie. I am scratching my vagina." That old lady nearly had a heart attack—she was outraged that my child knew that she had a vagina. Go figure.

I was twenty-two years old when I made the decision to freely have sex for the first time ever with a man I had been dating for about three months. I had been in the church all my life, baptized at twelve years old, and had my own Sunday school class. I loved church and I thought at that young age that I had a relationship with God, and yet when I turned twenty-two and was still very active in the church I fell deeply in love with this man. He was twenty-five, and I wanted to have sex with him. He was a kind, gentle, and loving man who knew that I was a virgin, and he never once tried to talk me into sex. He respected the fact that I was a church girl and just enjoyed going out with me. We had some really great times together. One day while watching television at his home, I got up, went to the rest room, and came back totally naked. I called his name, and he turned, looked at me, and still said, "Are you sure?" I said yes. This was supposed to be a scary time, a painful time, and I am supposed to have a horrible story to tell about my first time. Well, I don't. Yes it was scary, but it was also wonderful, not because I knew what I was doing, but because he did. I thank God (that's right) that after my childhood rape experiences, he allowed my first real sexual experience to be with a gentle, kind, and loving man who took time with me and taught me how wonderful and beautiful lovemaking could be. That is the story that I shared with my daughter; not to just wait until marriage, but—if you can't wait—to get to know who you are making this big step with and know that it can be a wonderful experience without the benefit of marriage. Once we became intimate, we also became creative. We made love on the table, under the Christmas tree, sitting in a chair; we showered together, and we still had fun just dating and been friends. We mutually agreed after about nine months to stop having sex and date other people and be friends. I must admit since this was my first time in a sexual relationship that I was hurt and saddened, but I am pleased to say that thirty years later he and I are still good friends. We have experienced marriage and parenthood, and we both are still very active in our individual churches.

So, as the mother of a beautiful, young fifteen-year-old girl, what is my point of view? First let me just say that I do not support teenagers having sex; I don't advocate for premarital sex, nor do I support masturbation as a form of hormonal control.

However, I'd gladly choose all of the above over teenage pregnancy, HIV and AIDS, venereal disease, abortion, dropping out of high school, and turning eighteen with three children on government assistance. My daughter and I see all these commercial and public service announcements on TV encouraging parents to talk to their children about sex and giving them different ways to do that. Still there are so many parents who find this subject not only difficult but also embarrassing to discuss, and I just don't get that. So my question becomes, what crap did you go through in your first and maybe even in your fifth or sixth sexual encounter, and why wouldn't you want to properly prepare your child with an open and honest conversation? Whether you are raising Christian, Jewish, or Islamic children—*talk to them!*

Open, honest conversation can be a blessing to them and healing for you, and you will be surprised at how they truly appreciate it. Why do we lie to our children?

We lie to them when we tell them this is not the time to have this conversation. We lie to them when we tell them to learn it in the street like I did. We really lie to them and ourselves when we tell them that we waited until marriage. Were you a natural virgin or a born again virgin on your wedding day? Why not be honest.

I think my first conversation with my daughter about sex came around the age of nine, but it was really innocent. She asked if kissing was a part of sex. What do you think? Some say kissing is a part of sex, and others say that it is not. I say it is if it leads to more than just kissing. Her actual question to me was, "Mommy, how does it feel to tongue kiss someone?" So I grabbed her, caught her off guard, and laid one on her. She quickly pushed me away and yelled, "*Gross!*" I said, "Good, remember that." She and I laughed until we were crying; she told me I was weird, but she loved me. I am pleased to say that since that time, she has asked me lots of questions: How does it feel to get your booty rubbed? How come boys like to touch your breasts? What is an orgasm? I answered every question openly, honestly, and without shame, and I didn't feel shocked, nor did I say "Let's talk about it later." I have no idea what she had heard or from whom, but I was cooking dinner and she came into the kitchen and simply said, "Mom, what is an orgasm?" Without missing a beat in my cooking, with no shameless grin or shock, I said the following:

When a man and woman are engaged in sexual intercourse, your hormones become very enlightened to one another's touch. If a man is kissing you and rubbing on your breasts, you might start to feel things that you have never felt before. If at some time he puts his hand in your panties and starts playing with your vagina, you will become excited to the point that your body expels fluids either from the vagina or, in his case, the penis, which gives you a sense of relief and feels really good.

I also told her that is why sex is reserved for married people, because you become so familiar with one another that you do not want anyone else doing those things to you. It is a special and magical time, and once you get started and have that kind of experience, it is only natural that you would want to continue to experience that more and more. I believe she was thirteen or fourteen when we had that talk. She later told me that she and two other friends had decided to ask their moms that question and come back to one another and compare answers. She shared that bit of information with me after they met back up at school and she learned that one of the girls was grounded and yelled at severely for asking that question and that the other girl's mom accused her of already having sex and took her cell phone away from her. She wanted to thank me for loving her enough to be honest. Some might say that what I shared was a bit much, but I say it was enough to let her know that I trust her with that information. After speaking to her other friends, she came away feeling special, loved, and respected. She felt like the information was heavy, and she didn't want to take my trusting her with that information for granted. We bonded in a special way, just like we did when she asked her father and me what an erection was. I think that he had a mild heart attack and sat frozen. I just started to talk and again told her what it was and why and how it happens. You may wonder why my daughter is asking all of these questions. My answer is that she is a teenager in the public school system, where kissing, hugging, and touching takes place between classes. Many of the girls are pregnant, have given birth, or are on birth control pills, and the boys are walking around with condoms in their pockets. How grateful and thankful I feel that she comes to me knowing that she will not be judged and that she will get the truth. Many have told me that she and I have a special relationship, and we do; she is my child, and I love her more than my own life. However, most importantly, she is a little lady and her body is telling her things. Kids at school, as well as the television, radio, and other outlets, are speaking volumes to her on a daily basis, and out of all that she hears, I want and need my voice to be the loudest.

ANNA

Anna is twenty-five years old and single. She is a very pretty lady by anyone's standards, and she sings like an angel. Anna is a born-again believer and a devoted Christian. She is one of the lead singers in the church choir and no doubt has an anointing on her voice to sing, but she has two major problems. The first problem is something she talks about quite often and carries a lot of guilt and shame about. She has been to counseling outside and inside of the church, but she and I are very close, so she shares the problem with me too. When she has a good day, we rejoice together, and when she doesn't, she beats herself up over it. Why do I do this? Why can't I control this demon? She has prayed and cried out to God for help, and when this subject or anything closely related to it comes up in a sermon, she is sure beyond a shadow of a doubt that the minister is talking to her. So many people—pastors, elders, ministers, and family members—know about this, and we all still love her and are there for her. Have you guessed what it is? Anna is a thief. The girl shoplifts clothes, jewelry, underwear, candy bars, and anything else she can get her hands on when she is in a store. Anna has never stolen from family, friends, or coworkers, but something about being in a store makes her want to steal. She has been caught and paid for the merchandise, as most of the time she has the money on her to do so. She has been placed on probation many times and, like

I said before, she goes to counseling. Let's continue to keep Anna in our prayers.

Anna's second problem is that she is single, saved, and having sex with a young man from the church who is also single and saved. Unlike the shoplifting, this issue doesn't bother her, but no one in church outside our small circle knows about it. She knows the people within the church will not love her, support her, and help her through this like they do the shoplifting, because as we all know, sex is a nasty little four-letter word that says you can't be saved, you can't be anointed, you can't love Jesus, and you need to step down from the choir until you are delivered.

So Anna has embraced this as her secret, and no one will know. I can hear you cursing me now; well, this is my story and Anna's problem, and I tend to see it as she does since I have seen this so many times in so many churches. If you are having sex outside the covenant of marriage, you are considered a horrible person. Sure, the church is willing to pray for you and with you, but at what cost? It's amazing how we rally around every conceivable problem there is with love and support gambling, lying, stealing, cheating (except on your spouse), poverty, pride, and jealousy, and have no problem keeping those secrets, but when it's about sex, we say "Lord, let's put him/her out of the church, I knew she/he was a fake or phony!"

What is it about sex that makes us go crazy? Why can't we love our leaders and church members through this like we can anything else? Satan was thrown out of heaven for having sex, right? Adam and Eve were cast out of the Garden of Eden for having sex, and Job lost all of his worldly possessions for having sex, right? *Wrong!* So where did this come from, and why are we born-again believers so afraid of dealing with this subject? People, we have got to get a grip on our sex issues. We allow our children to slip and fall in every area but sex, and that's why there is so much curiosity about it.

Can you count the many sermons you have heard on fornication, adultery, and lust? We are not beaten down on any other sin but this one. In fact, I don't recall a full message preached on the sin of lying, or lying being slipped into the sermon even just as a side note. Proverbs 6:16–19 in the New King James Bible reads as follows: "There are six things that the Lord hates, seven that are an abomination to him *haughty eyes, a lying tongue, and hands that shed innocent blood, a heart that devises wicked plans, feet that make haste to run to evil, a false witness who breathes out lies, and one who sows discord among brothers.*" Man, that chapter is a scary one that I recommend we all try to live by and not find ourselves caught up in; but it is amazing—nothing about having sex. Now, further down in that same chapter there is a warning against adultery and the possible consequences that it brings, but it is interesting at least to me that it is not listed as one of the seven things that the Lord hates. I know we all know God hates our sin and not the sinner, so why can't we act the same way since we claim that we are all Christ-like? People should hate the sin, not the sinner, and take the pressure off those who need a shoulder to cry on so they don't feel like they are out there alone.

DAVE

There's not much that I can say about Dave except that he is the one having regular and good sex with Anna. I don't really know Dave except what Anna has told me. I see him from time to time at service, and he appears to be a stand-up kind of guy. I have never heard gossip that he might have started about her and their relationship, so I guess he respects her and is aware of the huge problem this could cause for them both should the news get out. I have but one comment for him: continue to love her and treat her right, and if you love her, stop just having sex with her and marry the lady. But on the flip side, thanks for having protected sex.

Eight Years in a Gynecologist's Office

I have worked in three different gynecologist's offices for a total of eight years, and the things that I saw would probably not surprise you, but they would make you think *What in the world are these parents thinking?* If you have a minor female child who is having a normal monthly period, and you are the one doing all of the shopping and are responsible for purchasing her female products, tell me how in the hell you don't know that she is pregnant when you have not purchased those items for her in months? If you are the one purchasing her clothes and her clothes size keeps going up and you don't ask why, come on. I know girls in their teens like privacy and independence, but to what extent do you let them do their own thing? Do you never check the room when they are not home? Do you never go into the dressing room with them when trying on clothes? Do you not pay attention to their eating habits, illnesses, fatigue, and irritability all without reason? Has your life become so busy that you have totally checked out on her and then get mad when you learn that she is three to four months pregnant?

I say you should be mad at yourself. Do you know how many mothers don't even know that just because a girl is not having her menstrual cycle doesn't mean she can't get pregnant? Man, I can't tell you how many times I have heard, "She hasn't even started her period yet! How can she be pregnant?" My question is, why do you even have a child? There are many girls fifteen to twenty-one with vaginal warts, and they get upset not because they have this disease, but because they are afraid that the boy who gave it to them will leave them once he learns about it. It is crazy!

Yes, I am being hard, mean, and seemingly insensitive, but we have got to come to the realization that whether we are raising these girls in the church, temple, synagogue, or whatever, they are out there and they are having sex. We have got to stop this holier-than-thou approach to helping them deal with the strange and unexplained changes that are happening in their bodies and talk to them and prepare them to deal with this in a real non–Bible whipping way. None of us want our child, male or female, to become a teen parent, but when you have not spoken to them about sex, then they will explore. Even if you have had this talk, have you made them feel that they can come to you if they feel that they can't wait? Does your sixteen-year-old son feel comfortable asking you to go with him to purchase condoms? Does your daughter feel okay asking you for birth control pills without you looking at her like she's crazy and running her to the church for counseling and deliverance? Please don't get me wrong;

I am not saying you should stop parenting and become their friend, nor am I saying to support them becoming sexually active without the benefit of marriage. What I am saying is that you should be real, as real as possible, and open the door to raising them with a healthy respect for their bodies and a full knowledge and understanding of the decision they may make concerning premarital sex. Their understanding has to be a lot more than "It is against God's will and it's a sin." They need to know how wonderful and beautiful it can be to explore and share the body of the one you love once you are married and that it is the most precious gift that he or she can give. I can't help but wonder how much happier we all would have been and how many mistakes in sex we could have avoided if we had had an open, realistic, early approach to sex and intimacy before the "I do"s took place. Now here we are in our marriages some twenty plus years of later never having experienced an orgasm. One lady told me she had never had an orgasm until she had an affair and had no idea what was happening to her. Then there's the married man who had never had a woman on top until he had an affair and the lady took the lead and blew his mind when she climbed on top. These are people who had only one sexual partner in life, their spouse, and became curious after the age of fifty and started having an affair to see what the hype about sex was. They came to realize that they were missing passion and pleasure from their lives and didn't know how to get that from one another, so they went outside the marriage covenant and surprisingly enough were able to forgive one another and include the things they learned in to a healthy and stronger marriage. However, let's be real; that is not everybody's story, for adultery is the number-one reason for Divorce at least that what people say.

STATICS

I checked the CDC and many other health journals and news reports for this information. They are all out there on the Web so you can educate yourself as well as your children to help keep them safe, not only from teen pregnancy but also from the many sexually transmitted diseases they can contract.

- 1.2 million cases of chlamydia were reported in 2008.

- Nearly 337,000 cases of gonorrhea were reported that same year.

- Girls ages 15 to 19 had the most chlamydia and gonorrhea, at 409,531.

- Blacks make up 12 percent of the United States population, yet 71 percent have these diseases reported.

- 13,500 syphilis cases were reported in 2008.

- During 2004, 16,000 babies were born to girls aged 10 to 19 in Georgia alone, and of these births 3,400 were repeat births.

- Over ninety high school girls are pregnant at this moment in one high school, and many have had their second abortion.

I am sure you can find more recent data, and you should. You need to keep yourself abreast of these findings and speak to your children about them. There is some good news, which is that there has been a decline in the number of sexually transmitted diseases as well as the pregnancy rate; however, the numbers are still extremely high, and this is only from one of fifty states reporting.

www.cdc.gov

Vernice (Vern) Haliburton

Jordan's Spoken Word: Sex is Not Sexy

I want to but I don't. He
says it's okay but I won't.

That's not something I should
give away to someone I
might not see another day.
"Everyone's doing it," he tells
me. He continues saying that
it will fill me with glee. But
knowing I might contract a
STD, I decide to set him free.

Sex is not a game to play,
not once a week or any day.

It's bad enough without
a ring, but as a teen it's
a different thing.

Chapter 2

FOR THE CHEATING MARRIED PEOPLE

In doing my research on this subject, I learned that the three components that most successfully married people use to keep their marriages strong are the exact same ones that open the gateway to those who cheat. By the way, these people are married, saved, and having sex with someone other than their spouse.

THE GATEWAY

According to the New Webster Dictionary, a gateway is a way through the gate of some enclosure. In this section I will look at the three components of, or gateways into, cheating. I find it funny that the dictionary uses the word *enclosure,* which seems kind of binding and restrictive when describing a marriage, but then again, that might be yet another reason to cheat—to get free of that binding and restrictive feeling. Here are the three gateways:

1) **Lack of Finances**
2) **Lack of Communication**
3) **Lack of Sex**

Lack of Finances: When your money is funny and your change is strange; when there is more month than money and the eagle doesn't fly in time—the money wars begin. Adultery is expensive—the hotel rooms, the secret eating out, the little gifts that you buy for one another. You're broke at home and can't make ends meet, but somehow you find the money to cheat. What do you do when you can't pay your mortgage, the children need clothing, it's two days before payday, and there is nothing in the house to eat? You cheat, right? Wrong. I think that is the time to fill the communication gap. So many couples use this time to blame one another for the financial situation they are in. This is truly the time to sit down together and work out a financial plan and include the children in the process, depending on their ages. Here is another time when we block the kids out of communication as we do with the sex talk. We never let them know what is happening in the household. We leave them to figure out the silent treatment and fights on their own, and believe me, what they come up with is never anywhere near the real problem. I am not saying that the children need to be made aware of the full details of your money problems, but I feel if they are included it takes the pressure off wondering what is going on with Mom and Dad. You would be surprised how helpful and understanding they will be when you make them a part of things. For example, if they need new shoes, they need to know that it is okay to pay less for that shoe this time or maybe even put off buying shoes so that the family can get groceries. So many of our children are walking around with seventy- to one-hundred-dollar tennis shoes on their feet but are failing in their grades at school. How about making those eighty-dollar shoes an award for a passing grade for the semester instead of just allowing your kids to keep up with the latest trends. I am sure we are all aware by now that the Joneses not only are broke but also went into foreclosure and filed bankruptcy twice in the last twenty years. So why are we still trying to impress them? In my opinion, a lot of our financial problems are directly associated with our lack of communication.

So now you are not talking to one another, and when you do talk you fight. You are both frustrated over the bills, over not being able to take a vacation, and that the kids can't participate in school activities, and everyone is unhappy, so you or he finds someone outside the marriage to talk to. That venting to the opposite sex may have been very innocent in the beginning, but the gateway is slowly creeping open, and before you know it you have found someone who seemingly doesn't have a financial issue and is willing to treat you to a lunch for no reason. Now, though you used to be too tired to walk in the park and talk to your spouse, you find the time to sneak off to a hotel to rest in his arms away from the money wars. It's not that you want to be in an affair, it's because he listens to your voice, your pain; your need to be heard is being met, and somehow a sexual encounter rears its ugly head and you just let it happen. You're looking for that feeling of belonging, that intimacy and closeness that you long for and that your spouse doesn't seem to care about giving anymore.

As for him, women, we know we are always willing to listen, especially if it is a well-spoken gentlemen who needs to vent, and lo and behold this man never says one bad thing about his wife; he really loves her and wants the best for her. He is just missing that something that he can't put his finger on, and if his wife would be willing to fulfill that one piece of him that is missing, he would not be there with you. Ladies, you love that he wants to hear what you have to say and that your ideas matter, and again, somehow, the sexual encounter appears, and you are so tired of everything else that you have to deal with that you allow it to happen. I don't believe anyone, male or female, wakes up and thinks, *Today I am going to start an affair,* nor do I believe anyone wants to intentionally break his or her marriage vows. It's that damn gateway that needs protecting. Better yet, you need to have a spring door in your relationship. I looked up the word *spring,* and it has many different meanings. The two I love are "A time of season when things begin to grow," and "An elastic body made up of various materials." How great are those! Look at a your marriage as a constant time of growth, never ending growth that uses various materials to help it grow, such as counseling, marriage classes, open communication, trust, mutual love and respect, and prayer without feeling like you are in a restrictive situation. The lack of money may not ever completely go away in the course of your marriage, but how wonderful it would be to work together as a team to get to a place where you can control it and not have it control you.

Lack of Communication: No one is talking, and when you do, it is ugly. Or better yet, you talk all the time about everybody and everything except what is really bothering you. Check this one out: what do you do when you are talking about the problems you feel the marriage has and the other person is clueless? What do you do when you want out and your partner is happily married? No one is perfect, and there is no such thing as the perfect marriage. We hear all the time that marriage is hard, but is it? Does marriage have to be hard, or can we find a way to coexist with one another and both be happy. I say we both can be happy, and I say marriage doesn't have to be hard work. We make marriage hard, and we put undue pressure on ourselves mostly because we are trying to live up to someone's standard or live according to a religious belief instead of finding that peace and place within us as individuals and sharing that with the people we are married to. How many books on marriage have you read, or how many marriage seminars have you attended and gone home from and said to yourself, *We don't do any of that*? Then you turn your household upside down trying to incorporate these newfound principals into your marriage and do nothing but create a mess. My opinion is just that, and what works for me may not work for you, so stop trying to imitate what you think I have or what you think you see, for we all know that looks are deceiving. No one knows what's going on behind closed doors but the two that are living it. Just because a couple has been married for twenty years doesn't mean they are or ever were happily married. I personally know of a couple that has been married for twenty-eight years, and he was in an affair for five of those years and she is going on her tenth year in her affair. He was found out, but she hasn't been yet, and they think that their four children don't know. They still have wonderful dinner parties at their home, they travel together on vacation, and they just look good together, and so many people envy them. But she is so tired of him and wants him out of her life, and he doesn't understand why. She has tried to tell him, but she said it in an angry, nasty, and hateful way, so he thinks she was just having a bad day and taking it out on him. He thinks she has forgiven him and things are back to normal. It is one of the strangest marriages I know of, and yet some of the friends on the outside really think they want what this couple has. Why do we make this vow until death do us part, but want out when the minute things are no longer working? We don't want to die to get out, so where did that phrase come from and how do we get so wrapped up in it? Are we really in love with that person when we get married, or are we in love with love and wrapped up in the wedding? When you talk to people who have been married thirty years or more, they tell of how hard it was in the beginning and how many times they thought about leaving. They say how they thought they would never make it, but through prayer and other methods they have gotten past that and now it's good. Those who are past that mark really feel that it is the best part of their marriage. Is it the love of love or the love of that person that has kept them in it? In my research I have found that it is the children or the covenant that they made. Honoring the covenant until death seems to outweigh everything else, and somehow that keeps them moving forward. I sat down one day and personally made a list of all the reasons I should and need to divorce my current husband. By the time I got to number twenty-five, my heart was aching, not because of the length of the list but because there was so much more that I wanted to add. So on the next page I decide to make a list of reasons to stay, and lo and behold, my covenant vows were number one and my daughter was number two. Those two things were way more powerful than the other side. I tried to add love, friendship, companionship, security, and all those other things to the list and realized that I have those already in many other relationships. So I removed them and again was left with the covenant and came to realize that everything we need is in that covenant agreement. Then why can't we talk? Why don't we see eye to eye or even agree to disagree? Why can't we push past all the bad and make it to thirty plus years, when it is all supposed to get so good? This is the world of technology, and people who've been married thirty years now didn't have to deal with the Internet, Twitter, text messaging, e-mail, Facebook, or any of those other outlets that have taken away from that good, old-fashioned face-to-face time.

Lack of Sex: When there is too much sex for one and not enough sex for the other person, you not only create for yourself a gateway but you also create a tsunami. What is enough sex, and what determines not enough, and how did we get here? In the Bible it says that in marriage all things are honorable and the bed is undefiled. Does that mean you are supposed to do whatever your partner wants whenever he wants, or does it mean you have a mutual agreement of what, when, or how often you come together in sex and what exactly that activity will entail? The Bible also tells us that upon marriage our bodies are no longer ours but that they belong to the other person, and except for times of agreement we are not to deprive the other person. So again, does that mean your spouse gets to do whatever, whenever with you and you are supposed to take it because you said "till death do us part?" I said forsaken all others and clinging only unto them. The marriage vows are powerful, and I believe a part of the premarital classes that you attended (at least I hoped you attended) really took time and broke down those vows and opened you up to a real discussion. Ours didn't. He was wonderful, funny, and asked a lot of questions about how we felt about each other, what attracted us to each other, what we wanted out of the marriage, whether we were planning on having kids, and who would handle the finances and how, but never once did he break down and make us take a long, hard look at the wedding vows. He did ask if he wanted us to take out the promise to obey part, and of course I did. My husband and I had a vow renewal at fifteen years, and part of those vows stated, and I quote, "May God deal ever so severely with me should I choose to leave you." That scared the hell out of me, and I just barely mumbled those words under my breath. I didn't want to say that, nor did I feel I deserved that should I want to leave this marriage. The fact of the matter is that people change and things happen whether we intentionally allow them or not. How many men have started affairs because their wives have gotten obese after having children? They didn't or couldn't lose the weight and just kept gaining and the husband got turned off. He still loved his wife and wanted to stay with her, but he also wanted a smaller woman to make love with. Men get potbellies or overwork themselves so that sex and intimacy becomes a chore rather than a pleasure, and the woman can sense when they are just having sex without any real connection to her. I personally hate planned sex. Don't say to me, "Let's fool around," "Are you in the mood," or "How about we get together later after the kids are asleep." That is an instant turnoff for me. I like to be made love to all day long from the moment we wake in the morning, with that first good-morning kiss on the cheek, to cleaning up the breakfast dishes, to telling me all day that I am loved and beautiful. It's the little things all day long that say "Baby, I got you; you are important and special to me. I only want to spend time with you." What happens at night when you get in the bed is the climax to the lovemaking that has taken place all day. You can't go all day with no interaction and expect to receive intimacy at night. The same goes for the woman—romance him all day long with love texts, compliments, and more. Go to bed looking like you want to be touched. Even if you are carrying extra weight, make yourself appealing so he sees beyond the weight to the person you are inside. We have become so comfortable with the lack of sex that even if cheating is going on we could care less or develop the attitude that two can play that game. The funny part is that we are happily married and saved people.

Signs of Infidelity

These are not mine, and I don't necessarily agree with them. They are just some of the ones that I found and that other people have shared with me. With the exception of the first one listed, they are not in any particular order. They are informational only.

1. **Becoming emotionally unattached.** A person starts acting like he or she is single and loses interest in things at home. (I disagree with this being the number-one reason. There could be a number of other issues taking place that have nothing to do with someone cheating; however; this could also be a

big sign. When I was diagnosed with lupus, I became all about myself. I spent all my time on the Internet surfing for information, going to wellness seminars, and meeting other people with the illness; I closed myself off from my husband and child. Dealing with this was very personal and private, until I gathered my data and was able to include my husband. What a mess it would have been if he had thought that I was cheating just because I pulled away during that time.)

2. **Becoming mean and hateful toward the other person.** Women are moody, though some more than others and some at only certain times of the month. I believe men can be moody as well, and this may or may not be a sign of infidelity. Don't jump to conclusions; check it out. (In

today's economy, things are really tight for a lot of people. Where there were two jobs in the home, now there may only be one or none. The soaring gas prices are taking away from the household budget, and many people find they have little or no patience for no apparent reason.) There could be some cheating going on, maybe an emotional affair where someone else is making the cheater feel things that he or she no longer gets from his or her spouse by offering praise, compliments, and appreciation. Please check it out with facts and don't rely on what you feel, as we all know our feelings can easily let us down.

3. **Taking better care of oneself; paying attention to looks.** Maybe your spouse is losing weight or wearing cologne or

buying new clothes. (I have to say that you are nuts if you think your spouse is cheating just because he or she is taking better care of himself or herself.) I have been on my husband for years to lose weight after many sicknesses and hospitalizations for various reasons. He would lose a lot of weight and look super fine, but as soon as he was all better he would put that weight back on, and it was a huge turnoff to me. I let him know in no uncertain terms that I was not attracted to him and all that weight, but it never bothered him over the years. Now lately he is for some reason working hard on eating right, eating light, working out, and trying to take better care of his overall health and well-being. I say it's about damn time, but I don't think he's cheating.

4. **Private cell phone usage.** Here is another sign of the times. Many of the numbers in my husband's phone belong to women, and I don't know the majority of them. (Life is too short for me to being worrying about who he is calling and who all those women are. The fact of matter is that he had many female friends prior to our marriage, so why should the words "I do" change that for him?) There is no password on his phone, and I have answered it many times when it has rang. Some women will acknowledge me and state who they are; some are stupid and have not and just asked for him. *I don't care.* There are TV shows that follow a suspected cheating spouse, and some have used their own private investigator, gone through

pockets, checked cell phone records, and called the spouse's place of employment. *What the hell!* There is no way I am going through all of this. Baby, if you think I am cheating physically or have become emotionally involvement with someone else, just ask—save the time and money. If you do ask and think you have been lied to, then start the hard stuff if you must. As for me, life is too short. I just don't have the time, money, or energy.

There are many more signs, and most can be debated as fact or fiction. I have neither the time nor energy to deal with them all. Some would say that I have a very naive view on the cheating of a spouse, and others would say it is a very healthy view. The truth of the matter is that I don't care; I really don't. Do you know how much time and energy it takes to try to figure out whether your spouse is cheating or not? You can hire a professional to find out for you, or you can snoop around on your own, but I believe that you first have to be open and honest with yourself. You have to take a cold, hard look at your gateway and see if there are any open doors or even a crack in the window that might allow for adultery to creep in. If for some reason it is discovered and proven, now what do you do? Is divorce the answer, or can you work your way back through this betrayal, hurt, and pain? As for me, cheating is not a deal breaker or cause for divorce, though bringing home an outside child and/or disease is.

STATISTICS:

- Fifty percent of all marriages will end in divorce.
- Extramarital affairs happen in Christian marriages.
- Seventy percent of women in

physically abusive relationships are not cheating.

- Sixty percent of marriages that end in divorce do so because of finances or the illness of a partner, not cheating,

- Your spouse can show all the signs of cheating and not be cheating. He or she can also show no signs at all and be actively involved in an affair.

AND THE ANSWER IS ...

Did you seriously think that you were going to get to the end of this book and find an answer? This entire book is based on one woman's opinion, and what works for me may or may not work for you.

In regard to the children, I absolutely stick to my guns about having an open, honest, straightforward talk with your children about sex. No beating around the bush, no sugar coating. Just give them not only what they want but what they need, which is you and a real look into what you think and feel about this subject. The bottom line is that you can raise your children in the best of households with or without religious influence (I personally feel it should be with), but they are going to do what they want to do, so why not educate them and empower them to make good decisions? If, God forbid, my child becomes a teenage mom, it will not be because she couldn't talk to me or because she feared how I would respond. She as already spoken to me, and she knows what I feel and think and what I want for her and her future, which is the absolute best. I want her to finish college with at least a master's and marry and have a family with a saved, actively involved Christian man. That is my dream for her. It may or may not be the future she wants for herself. Life has a funny way of going in the opposite direction you think it will go.

Now for the cheating and saved people—I can but only say marriage and a mortgage. *Don't believe the hype.* The two big *M*s can become the biggest pain in the place where you sit if you are not again open and honest with yourself and your spouse. I was speaking to a friend who is currently married, saved, and having an affair. This person told me that she wanted to get married so badly that she said whatever sounded good during their premarital classes. Now she knows that her spouse was lying as well, because they both are now having problems, are actively involved in affairs, and are holding fast to those vows.

Marriage truly should not be entered into lightly, and neither should the purchase of a home. I feel so bad for these families nowadays that are losing their homes because of job loss, illness, and other legitimate causes. So many people got in over their heads because someone told them that home ownership was God's will or that they had to get out of their apartment and start a family after getting married.

I think I do have the answers: Be honest with yourself first and foremost. Then and only then can you be truly honest with your spouse and offspring. You should know yourself, love yourself, be open with yourself, and live for yourself without allowing too much of who you are to be heavily influenced by another.

About the Author

Vernice (Vern) Haliburton, author of *Breathing Under Water, Believe It or Not You are Not Alone,* and *The Seeds You Sow,* is a wife and mother. She currently lives in Conyers, Georgia, and spends all of her spare time with family and friends. She is a very magnetic writer.

CPSIA information can be obtained
at www.ICGtesting.com
Printed in the USA
FFOW04n2117150117
31397FF